LIMERICKS IN THE TIME OF TRUMP

D1606228

LIMERICKS
in the TIME of
TRUMP

A Collection by the
Previously Gruntled Poets

Lindsay Crane, Stephen Benko,
Phil Graham, and Zelda Dvoretzky

Compiled and Edited by
Lindsay Crane

Foreword by
Anu Garg

Print and Pixel Books
Lafayette, California

This book may be ordered from Amazon, BarnesandNoble.com, and PrintandPixelBooks.com, in print and electronic versions.

Crane, Lindsay. *Limericks in the Time of Trump*
ISBN (softcover): 978-0-9833051-5-6
ISBN (ebook): 978-0-9833051-6-3

Art by Ivor Tosic (IvorTosicArt@gmail.com)
Book design by Blue Star Presse

Published by Print and Pixel Books
Lafayette, California
Printed and bound in the United States of America

Publisher's Cataloging-in-Publication

Names: Crane, Lindsay, author. | Benko, Stephen, author. |
Graham, Phil, author. | Dvoretzsky, Zelda, author.
Title: Limericks in the time of Trump : a collection by the previously gruntled poets / Lindsay Crane , Stephen Benko , Phil Graham , Zelda Dvoretzky ; compiled and edited by Lindsay Crane.
Description: Includes index. | Lafayette, CA: Print and Pixel Books, 2017.
Identifiers: ISBN 978-0-9833051-5-6 (pbk.) | 978-0-9833051-6-3 (ebook)
Subjects: LCSH Trump, Donald, 1946---Humor. | Presidential candidates--United States--Humor. | Presidents--United States--Election--2016--Humor. | Political culture--United States--Humor. | United States--Politics and government--Humor. | Limericks. | BISAC HUMOR / Form / Limericks & Verse | HUMOR / Topic / Politics
Classification: LCC PN6231.T735 .C73 2017 | DDC 811.6—dc23

Contents

Foreword

THE RESULTS OF THE 2016 election told schoolboys across America, if you work hard and call that special needs kid a "retard" and steal lunch money from that bookish kid and ping the bra strap of the girl sitting in front of you and trip that lanky kid on the playground, one day you too can be the president of the United States.

Well, it looks like pettimanus* is the new president of the United States. Little men are now casting big shadows. Even small hands can do big damage.

What can we do? The first step would be to tell it like it is and call them out and not be afraid to speak up, as limericists in this book do. Also, write, share, speak, march, and run. Run as in run for an office, for city council, for school board, for state representative. Even small steps can go long distances if we keep going.

~ Anu Garg, Founder of Wordsmith.org

---

* Literally, "small hands," but you could also interpret the word as "petty man" or "little man."

Introduction

As the proud creators of pungent limericks about the 2016 election, the authors of this slim volume decided we must fulfill our obligation to humanity by sharing our work with the millions of people around the world who are appalled, aghast, sickened, horrified, shocked, and repulsed by the results.

We met on Anu Garg's marvelous website and newsletter, A Word A Day (AWAD, at www.wordsmith.org). Each day Anu posts an unusual word, with its definition, derivation, and usage in a quotation from a book, magazine or newspaper, and adds an unrelated philosophical thought for the day. Hundreds of thousands of faithful followers enjoy this daily ritual of logophilia.

Enter Steve Benko, a long-time AWAD subscriber who began composing limericks using the day's word as a mental calisthenic each morning after retiring from a corporate middle-management career. These limericks began to turn more and more acerbically political when Trump announced his candidacy and it began to gain momentum. Phil Graham, retired computer consultant, sometime composer, and irrepressible punster, enthusiastically did the same, though on his own limerick blog and without necessarily using the AWAD words. Zelda Dvoretzky, our fearless octogenarian, who remembers Pearl Harbor and cast her first vote for Adlai Stevenson, then joined in, showing us that the horror of Drumpf (his actual ancestral family name) was international in scope.

We thus began this book project, largely for our own mental health and the amusement of our friends. I suggested it, whereupon Steve, that fountain of verses, leaped into action and produced the following,

"Let's publish a book!" said Ms. Crane.
Answered Steve, "Well, the timing's germane."
    Then Zelda and Phil
    Said, "It sure beats a pill.
This could save us from going insane!"

Yes, this is serious insanity prevention. The psychological term is "Sublimation," which in this sense means turning pain into something useful or (arguably) artistic. Activism falls into this category, so protests and the like can be signs of robust mental health. Sublimation and Humor are two of the healthiest psychological defense mechanisms.

Phil is an old hand in this art form, and penned the following:

The limerick rarely disguises
Itself as a poem worth prizes.
    I have written a few
    And have learned it is true
That the good ones' last lines have surprises.

Demonstrating that limerick artistry is partly genetic, Phil's brother, Steve Graham, contributed the following (the last line of which I've edited):

Meritorious books feature forewords
Authors list *raisons d'être* and core words.
    But when all's said and done
    Readers jump to Page One
And ignore those superfluous snore words.

Phil also found this gem in the public domain:

The limerick, peculiar to English,
Is a verse-form that's hard to extinguish.
    Once Congress in session
    Decreed its suppression,
But people got around it by writing the last line without any rhyme or meter.

Not an AWAD follower? We've provided Anu's definitions for the words he highlighted in his column, and some other definitions for words we, in our diabolical way, chose ourselves.

Want to join us in this act of literary resistance? Just buy copies and give them to your friends. That would qualify as Altruism, the third in the triumvirate of healthy responses to horrible news.

~ Lindsay Crane, psychologist and
newly minted limerophile

Hors d'oeuvre:

Folly Even Before the Tournament Begins

~ 1 ~

Purblind (PUHR blind)
*Partially blind, or lacking
in understanding or insight*

When I need to relax and unwind
I must dial my brain to "purblind,"
    And turn a deaf ear
    This political year
Or I'll surely go out of my mind.

~ 2 ~

Blag
*To obtain something by guile; to cheat,
rob, snatch, steal, scam, or beg*

Pols who think an election's a blag
Mouth inanities wrapped in the flag.
    Just to get into power
    They'll lie by the hour.
It's enough to make anyone gag.

~ 3 ~

Gnomic
*Puzzling or incomprehensible
yet seemingly profound*

"In our families is where wings take dream,"
One fine day was George Dubya's theme.
    The talk can be gnomic
    Down by the Potomac
But that time I wanted to scream.

~ 4 ~

Fane
A place of worship

At a right-wing evangelist fane
They prefer that you not use your brain.
    But "Science and reason
    To Jesus are treason"?
That's taking the Lord's name in vain.

~ 5 ~

BLAG
*To obtain something by guile; to cheat,
rob, snatch, steal, scam, or beg*

"I'll wave the American flag,
And call Hillary Clinton a nag,"
    Says the Donald, "This deal
    To do condos is real
For the White House I'm soon gonna blag."

~ 6 ~

ESTIVATE (antonym of hibernate)
To pass the summer in a dormant state

Said Dubya, "This summer I'll estivate,
Chop wood on my ranch, and holes excavate.
    It's time to relax,
    For Saddam got the axe.
That'll teach him to misunderestimate."

11

Before
the Nominations:
The Dunciad

The Complacent Cruz
See Limerick #16

~ 7 ~

HYPOGEAL (hy-puh-JEE-uhl)
Living, growing, or existing underground

He lives high in a tower of steel
But belongs in a lair hypogeal.
 From under Trump's rock
 He could harmlessly mock
All the rights that he'd like to repeal.

~ 8 ~

PASSEL
A large number

Said the counselor, "Admission's no hassle,
And our courses? Trump U. has a passel!
 You pay our tuition
 And dreams reach fruition!
So who needs a cap, gown, and tassel?"

~ 9 ~

PRECARIOUS
Risky, uncertain, insecure, unstable, unsafe

"My wives have been many and various,"
Says Trump, "And it's always precarious.
    From Pisces to Taurus
    They nag like a chorus.
Next time I should try Sagittarius."

~ 10 ~

ARGLE-BARGLE
A noisy dispute or discussion; nonsense

Have Republicans lost all their marbles?
Their debates were just big argle-bargles.
    All night they'd assert
    Ugly falsehoods and dirt,
And the winner some toxic brew gargles.

~ 11 ~

Peculate
*To steal or misuse money or property
entrusted to one's care*

When Republicans cry out, "Deregulate!"
It's time for Wall Streeters to peculate.
    They pillage with glee
    Shouting "'Bye, SEC!"
While a finger they use to gesticulate.

~ 12 ~

Siren song
*An enticing appeal that
ultimately leads to disaster*

While the wealthy are playing badminton
It's "Revive Reaganomics" they're hintin'.
    Please don't play along
    With that old siren song.
Vote for Bernie, or Hillary Clinton.

~ 13 ~

STUMP
To campaign for office

What is it that makes Donald Trump
Hate illegals and be such a grump?
   Though NBC dropped him
   That act never stopped him
From planning to go out and stump.

~ 14 ~

HERD
A multitude of people, usually pejorative; a rabble

The Republicans seem rather blurred—
All those hats in the ring are absurd.
   But one thing's for damp sure,
   The folks in New Hampshire
Will help us by thinning the herd.

~ 15 ~

Hack
Low-level political operative,
usually with flexible morals

The gentleman doctor, Ben Carson,
Seems quiet and sweet like a parson.
    No political hack
    But he surely would lack
Enough moxie to shine like Greer Garson.

~ 16 ~

Schmooze
To chat idly; gossip

That conservative tea-bagger, Cruz,
When he opens his mouth, has to schmooze.
    Looks and talks like a pastor
    He'd be a disaster.
Oh my, how I hope that he'll lose.

~ 17 ~

Prowess
Superior skill, ability, or strength

The toes of the church ladies curled
At the prayer that the Donald unfurled.
    "O Lord, please endow us
    With sexual prowess
Sufficient to screw the whole world."

~ 18 ~

Mumpish
Sullen, silent, depressed

The Donald will surely grow mumpish
One day when Melania's plumpish.
    "Don't copy or model
    That Rosie O'Donnell,"
He'll say, "For that's not being Trumpish."

~ 19 ~

Frabjous
Wonderful, delightful

"Bernie Sanders is playing with matches.
In securities fraud he may catch us!"
    The thought of his axe
    Really scares Goldman Sachs,
But the rest of us find it quite frabjous.

~ 20 ~

Slithy (SLY-thee)
Smooth, slimy, slithery

O Lord, let Ted Cruz never ply thee
With prayers that are hateful and slithy.
    Down here we guffaw
    That he studied the law
At a school in the league known as Ivy.

~ 21 ~

SHEEPLE
*People who unquestioningly accept what's said by a
political leader, marketer, preacher, etc.*

Republicans speak to their sheeple
Like monkeys who fling matter fecal.
From skyscrapers Trump
Will his bucketsful dump,
While Ted Cruz throws it off of a steeple.

~ 22 ~

CHICANE (shih KANE)
Trick or deception

It seemed like some sort of chicane
When the Donald began his campaign.
Now he's grown like a bubble
His tactics as subtle
As Russia invading Ukraine.

~ 23 ~

CHICANE (shih KANE)
Trick or deception

We thought it must be a chicane
When Ms. Palin was picked by McCain.
    Did the man want to lose?
    But now Donald and Cruz
Make us wish for the ditz with no brain.

~ 24 ~

DEBENTURE
A certificate acknowledging a debt

To those who'd invest in his ventures
The Donald would hand out debentures.
    Said he, "You'll be rich
    Like Ivana, the bitch."
They're still waiting—by now they have dentures.

~ 25 ~

Gnarly
Slang for unpleasant or ugly

Which candidate will we next dump
So that fewer will stand on the stump?
    Prob'ly Kasich or Carly
    Though neither's as gnarly
As whom I'd like gone—Donald Trump.

~ 26~

Performative
*Relating to a statement that functions as
an action by being uttered*

When a candidate shouts out, "I promise!"
I suggest you be like Doubting Thomas.
    It may be performative
    But not so informative
For most of them aren't very honest.

After the Nominations:
Summer and Smokescreens

Trash talking at its trashiest
See Limerick #36

~ 27 ~

SHAFT
Mistreatment

Hil's the nominee, Prez she may gain.
She may finally break that glass pane!
    For Liz Warren, the shaft
    'Cause Ms. Clinton did draft
The Virginian—her Citizen Kaine.

~ 28 ~

HILARITY
Cheerfulness, merriment

Both Clinton and Trump have a charity
But between them there's no similarity.
    "Let's treat HIV"
    Or "Buy pictures of me."
It's so sad that it's almost hilarity.

~ 29 ~

WROTH
Extremely angry
TROTH
Belief, fidelity, truth

"I'll make everyone hateful and wroth,"
Swears the Donald, "For this is my troth.
    I have all the solutions
    Who needs Constitutions?
I'll whip the whole world to a froth."

~ 30 ~

FLATULATE
To pass intestinal gas

If the Donald is whom you would emulate
You needn't speak words, you just flatulate.
    "Debating's an art,"
    He says, "Just like a fart,
The whole room with my gases I inundate."

~ 31 ~

QUIXOTE
*Someone who is unrealistic, naïve, chivalrous,
idealistic, etc., to an absurd degree*

Never mind you're a sweet old Quixote.
If smuggled in by a coyote,
    With kicks in the rump
    "You're a rapist!" cries Trump,
Like a demon with pitchfork and goatee.

~ 32 ~

CHUTZPAH
Audacity, insolence, arrogance

Trump campaigns with chutzpah and swagger
And his weapons—the lie and the dagger.
    He comes from TV
    To rule you and me,
And that makes him a real carpetbagger.

~ 33 ~

BUSHWA
Nonsense, bulls***

Says Ivanka, "Yes, Jewish I am,
But my Dad isn't part of the clan.
  He spouts so much bushwa
  We know he's got chutzpah.
The trouble is that he's a ham."

~ 34 ~

LIEN
*A claim on another's property until
a debt owed by that person is paid back*

Says the Donald to girls of eighteen,
"Miss Piggy, I'd try Lean Cuisine."
  He continues on Twitter,
  "Her clothes do not fit her,
She's HUGE, like a Trump Tower lien!"

~ 35 ~

Laissez-faire
A hands-off policy, especially by government towards business

"In business we think laissez-faire
Would soon rescue the world from despair.
    The proper solution
    Is smoke and pollution.
We can't afford breathable air."

~ 36 ~

Vituperative
Criticizing bitterly, scathing, abusive

"The secret to being communicative,"
Says Trump, "Is to keep it vituperative.
    What more need I know?
    My reality show
Proved that trash talk is highly remunerative."

~ 37 ~

Dog whistle
A coded message that seems innocuous
to the general public but has a
hidden meaning for the target audience

A demagogue needs a dog whistle:
"Love is kind," he may quote the Epistle.
    His followers know
    He means make Muslims glow
With the light of a nuclear missile.

~ 38 ~

Officious
Pompous or domineering,
eager to offer unwanted advice

"For using big words like 'officious,'"
Said the crime lord, "You'll sleep with the fishes.
    You Mexican judges
    All carry such grudges
The Donald and I think you're vicious."

~ 39 ~

Orotund
Pompous, bombastic

Calls for violence sure sour my palate
Trump thinks he will judge with a mallet.
    His words orotund
    Cry out for a fund
Which would get him removed from the ballot.

During the Campaign: The War of the Words

The squinting stalker
See Limerick #52

~ 40 ~

Ad hoc
Impromptu

Donald Trump often says things ad hoc
When he should in his mouth put a sock.
    But it's quite entertaining
    When wisdom he's feigning
While serving up sh** in a crock.

~ 41 ~

Mendacious
Dishonest; telling falsehoods

He's rapacious, mendacious, and mean;
The worst candidate there's ever been,
    He screws fellow man
    Every chance that he can.
On Trump Tower they should slap a lien.

~ 42 ~

ULULATE
To howl or hoot
PULLULATE
To sprout, breed or swarm

The truth becomes something to mutilate
As the Donald continues to ululate.
    Like a dog he attacks
    Without checking the facts,
And yet somehow his poll numbers pullulate.

~ 43 ~

DEROGATE
To disparage or belittle

To become a Republican heavyweight
You let civil discourse disintegrate
    Insult your opponents'
    Most private components
Just denigrate, deprecate, derogate.

~ 44 ~

INVECTIVE
*Insulting or abusive words or expressions;
vehement denunciation*

Of nasty invective he's master,
And I pray she won't let him get past her.
    He plays dirty and crude.
    He's incredibly rude.
For the country he'd be a disaster.

~ 45 ~

BOMBAST
Pretentious, pompous speech or writing

The air's full of political chatter.
Our eardrums with bombast they batter.
    Each utterance specious
    Brings comment facetious—
Be serious! Outcomes do matter.

~ 46 ~

FAÇADE
Superficial or artificial appearance

Disappointment you may well avert
If you're skeptical of a stuffed shirt.
    He may strut like a god
    But it's all a façade.
Look at Donald. Need I reassert?

~ 47 ~

HENCHMAN
A subordinate, especially one who engages in illegal activities for a powerful boss or criminal.

The behavior of Trump and his henchmen
In school would soon get them detention.
    Rod Serling would say
    Of this weird wacky fray,
"You have entered another dimension."

~ 48 ~

COMPORT
To conduct (oneself) or agree with

Shrugged the Donald, "Campaigning's blood sport;
With the truth there's no need to comport.
    Next stop is the Oval.
    I hope Karl Rove'll
Help find me some hacks for the Court."

~ 49 ~

FLOCCIPEND (FLOK si pend)
To regard as worthless

Shouts the Donald, "Go home and defriend
All the people real men floccipend!
    On Facebook we'll start
    Then, as deals are my art,
Constitutional rights I'll suspend!"

~ 50 ~

TONSORIAL
Of or relating to a barber or barbering

Mr. Trump, though I don't really care,
You should do something else with your hair.
    A tonsorial blunder
    But what goes on under
It; that's what drives me to despair.

~ 51 ~

COMB-OVER
Attempt to conceal a bald spot
by growing the adjacent hair long

Your comb-over's really absurd.
Makes you look like some weird tropic bird.
    Still, it goes with your face.
    By the way, in this race
May you place last, way second, or third.

~ 52 ~

Sage
Wise, showing good judgment

The press called the night's debate "major."
Don't think there's much doubt who seemed sager.
    Clinton proved she has graces
    Trump yelled and made faces
Interrupted, but couldn't enrage her.

~ 53 ~

Boodler
A person involved with corruption and bribery

"My opponent," says Trump, "was a boodler.
It says so whenever I google her.
    The internet's true
    And between me and you
I got slapped when I tried to canoodle her."

~ 54 ~

KOOL-AID
Something accepted without question

"By voters I won't be a fool made!"
The apricot-hair-colored mule brayed.
    "With brown folks and women,
    My prospects are dimmin',
They'd better start drinking the kool-aid!"

~ 55 ~

KOOL-AID
Something accepted without question

I've begun to be very afraid
That too many have drunk the kool-aid.
    And if Trump gets the job,
    Soon that same angry mob
Will to civilization put paid.

~ 56 ~

AMBISINISTROUS
Clumsy with both hands

When you're groping some girl or your mistress
It's a pain to be ambisinistrous.
    Writes Trump, "Santa, please,
    I get nowhere with these,
Give me hands that are bigly for Christmas."

~ 57 ~

DEFENESTRATION
To throw something or someone out the window

Democracy's defenestration
Began with attacks on menstruation.
    "She's not very clever,
    She bleeds from wherever,"
Said Trump, and became a sensation.

~ 58 ~

PROPINE (pro PEEN)
To give or tip

When the Donald is venting his spleen
His poor chauffeur he has to propine.
    For who else will listen
    When women he's dissin'
With language that's from the latrine?

~ 59 ~

CONFUTE
To prove to be wrong

Says the Donald, "You just can't confute
That in business I'm very astute.
    And with stardom I'm armed
    So that women are charmed
When I grab them in places hirsute."

~ 60 ~

Confute
To prove to be wrong

A fact-checker should be astute
Since her work is to all lies confute.
 But with Donald, the Grinch
 Her job is a cinch;
His acquaintance with truth is minute.

~ 61 ~

Demagogue
*A person who appeals to prejudices
and emotions to gain power*

When people are shouting, "You demagogue!"
It sounds to the Donald like "demigod."
 "But why only half?"
 He complains, "Do the math,
For they love me in church and in synagogue."

~ 62 ~

VITRIOL
Cruel, mean-spirited bitter criticism

Shouted Trump, overflowing with vitriol,
"So what if my taxes are trivial!
    I keep all my booty
    Because it's my duty
To give late-night comics material."

~ 63 ~

IMMOLATE
To sacrifice, especially by burning

"If nuclear weapons proliferate,"
Says Trump, "The whole Earth we may immolate.
    But look at the bright side
    Less carbon dioxide
And Mexicans surely won't immigrate."

~ 64 ~

RUMINATE
To think deeply upon

"When your bills pile up and accumulate,"
Says the Donald, "Don't worry or ruminate.
    On your debts just default
    Then some women assault
And your spirits will quickly rejuvenate."

~ 65 ~

GLIB
Readily fluent, often thoughtlessly,
superficially, or insincerely so

Both candidates came off as glib,
Although much which each said was a fib.
    While I'm a conservative
    Trump isn't deservative.
I can't stand the cut of his jib.

~ 66 ~

CONDIGN
Well-deserved, appropriate

"I'll behave in a manner condign,"
Says the Donald, "When victory's mine.
 Watch everyone faint
 When with buckets of paint
On the White House my name I enshrine."

~ 67 ~

REBUS
The graphic representation of a word or phrase

"The voters have brains like amoebas,"
Says the Donald, "Look how they believe us!"
 A finger will do
 To express his world view
For the middle one's quite a good rebus.

~ 68 ~

POTUS
President of the United States

Herr Trump's POTUS hopes we must bust
(How is it his hair's never mussed?)
 Else he'll build that damned wall
 Then all money recall
Reissued, "In Donald We Trust."

~ 69 ~

FLAGRANT
Conspicuously obvious, glaring, or offensive

The stuff that he says is so flagrant
He ought to be kept in the basement.
 Of truth this gorilla
 Speaks not a scintilla.
He thinks that his poop isn't fragrant.

Shock and Aww ...
Oh, How We Wish!

~ 70 ~

Jambalaya
A heterogeneous mixture

The Donald is like the Messiah
For those who don't like jambalaya.
    "A spicy, diverse
    Population's a curse,"
Says the soon-to-be washed-up pariah.

~ 71 ~

Foozle
To botch or bungle

Said the psychic to Trump, "You and Cruz'll
One day try to voters bamboozle.
    But let me continue
    It isn't within you
To win, for the whole thing you'll foozle."

Post-Election:
The Stages of Shock

Denial

~ 72 ~

Horror
*A shuddering feeling caused by something
shocking, terrifying, or morally repugnant*

I awoke to a feeling of horror.
The news says he's already more or
    Less won the campaign.
    "It's not true!" I maintain,
For of him I am such an abhorrer.

~ 73 ~

Vitriolic
Marked by cruel, mean-spirited bitter criticism

It seems that a speech vitriolic
Is effective in districts bucolic.
    Is that all you need
    In the system we heed?
The results seem beyond diabolic!

Fear

"My ideal!"
See Limerick #74

~ 74 ~

BROMANCE
*An intimate, non-sexual
relationship between two men*

Now it seems he's embracing Assad.
It's apparent the world has gone mad.
    Was there even a chance?
    There's that Putin bromance—
U.S. voters, I think we've been had.

~ 75 ~

VERACITY
Truthfulness

Do not question the Donald's veracity
Guys may come after you with tenacity.
    In his crowds of buffoons
    There are quite a few goons
Getting paid in a brown-shirt capacity.

~ 76 ~

Nefarious
Extremely wicked or villainous

Close your eyes when his deeds are nefarious.
Make believe that his jokes are hilarious.
    Be a yes-man. If not
    You'll be canned on the spot
'Cause a toady's position's precarious.

~ 77 ~

Narcissist
A person characterized by
excessive self-interest or self-love

The Donald's not only a narcissist
Our values he'd torch like an arsonist.
    Support he's recruitin'
    From Vladimir Putin?
I'm calm, but that's thanks to my pharmacist.

Catharsis

"I have the best ethics in the world, the greatest."
See Limerick #88

~ 78 ~

COULROPHOBIA
Fear of clowns

With just a bit more coulrophobia
O Donald, we would have got over ya.
    But into your circus
    You knew how to work us.
I think I might move to Mongolia.

~ 79 ~

YELP
To give a quick, sharp, shrill cry

Trump, crazy clear through to his gut,
Glued a frog to the top of his nut.
    A doc asked, "May I help?"
    The frog croaked out a yelp,
"Can you get this wart offa my butt?"

~ 80 ~

GRUFF
Surly, showing a harsh demeanor

Though the Donald seems somewhat less gruff
The transition will likely be rough.
    Nobody seems misty
    That he dumped Chris Christie
But V.P. Mike Pence? He's all fluff.

~ 81 ~

PREXY
Slang for president

"I gave Bushes and Clintons the gate.
It was 'yuge' and I managed it great!
    So the first female Prexy
    Will be hot, smart, and sexy;
Ivanka, it's yours on a plate!"

~ 82 ~

SHANNON
River in Ireland

Trump's strategist guy is Steve Bannon
Way far-right, he's a really loose cannon.
    He is ready to start,
    But I wish he'd depart
For his homeland and jump in the Shannon.

~ 83 ~

TWIT
Foolish person

We've elected a prez who's a twit
And many don't like it one bit.
    With Chief of Staff Priebus
    Plus Bannon, so griebous,
It's like dental work—Reince and spit.

~ 84 ~

Keynes
*Economist who advocated that government
increase spending and reduce taxes
in response to an economic depression*

Besides the fact Don is a jerk
In his brains naught from Keynes seems to lurk.
    With his damned fickle frown
    He'll propose "trickle-down
Economics." Been tried. Didn't work.

~ 85 ~

Slur
*Insult, particularly an uncomplimentary
reference to another person's race*

Trump's filling his cabinet fast.
Blacks and Muslims will be more harassed.
    Named his A.G. Jeff Sessions,
    Who should make confessions
For racial slurs said in the past.

~ 86 ~

LEECH
Blood-sucking worm-like invertebrate;
person who parasitically profits off others

Of the Donald I'm wanting no part
I've never considered him smart.
    He's really a leech
    Can we please now impeach?
For he's thoroughly heartless at heart.

~ 87 ~

APACE
Quickly

With these earthquakes arriving apace
And weird weather all over the place,
    "Global warming's a hoax,"
    Our new president jokes.
"Crooked media's making the case."

~ 88 ~

Decalogue
The Ten Commandments

What's the best way to counsel a demagogue?
It's too late. He won't learn from a pedagogue.
    His ethics are small
    He's forgotten them all,
With no concept of even the Decalogue.

~ 89 ~

Catharsis
Release of unbearable emotional tension; purification

You notice our language is crude.
Some people might think it seems rude.
    But we all need catharsis
    Or else this darn farce is
Too stressful for me and my brood.

Resignation

~ 90 ~

KAKISTOCRACY
Government by the least qualified or worst persons

There are countries enduring autocracy,
Kleptocracy, even theocracy.
　　But being creative
　　We've chosen a state of
The latest new trend: Kakistocracy.

~ 91 ~

NITTY-GRITTY
The essential, practical, or most important details

Let's get to the real nitty-gritty.
The Donald will never admit he
　　Has fingers so small
　　But I don't care at all
For his heart is the thing itty-bitty.

Irrational Optimism

~ 92 ~

AGHAST
Struck with overwhelming
amazement, shock, or dismay

Though his racism leaves me aghast
As he charges full speed to the past,
    We will bravely resist
    Till he bursts like a cyst.
We'll be healthier after the blast.

~ 93 ~

GONALD
Gone, disappeared. The devout hope
of sane citizens of America and the world

The GOP gave us "The Donald."
Too bad he's not charming like Ronald.
    That's Reagan—quite nice—
    But his tax cuts failed twice.
Let's hope in four years Don is "gonald."

Resolution and Vigilance

~ 94 ~

Right
Conservative wing of a political party.
Derived from the seating of representatives in the
legislative chamber during French Revolution.

20/20 denotes perfect sight,
Though it wasn't displayed by the Right.
    2020, the year,
    If we'll all still be here,
Work could start towards a future more bright.

~ 95 ~

Defenestration
To throw something or someone out the window

Though some heard the results with elation,
I considered self-defenestration.
    But through fury and tears
    And four horrible years
We must strive for amelioration.

~ 96 ~

Confute
To prove to be wrong

His claims we can quickly confute
They're farcically fast to refute.
    Though his vict'ry's outrageous
    Wisdom's much more courageous.
My anger I'll try to transmute.

~ 97 ~

Grump
Discontented complainer

How to live through the era of Trump
Without turning us into a grump:
    We'll spread hope and love
    And with help from above
We will mindfully outlast that chump.

~ 98 ~

Bamboozle
To trick or cheat

You think you've bamboozled us all
With your promise of building that wall.
    But we'll be observing,
      You're crass and self-serving.
"Impeach!" we'll be ready to call.

~ 99 ~

Antepenultimate
Next to next to last

I was tempted to holler and curse,
Thinking, "Rats! It could hardly get worse."
    Then to me it occurred,
      "An encouraging word
Fits our antepenultimate verse."

~ 100 ~

Penultimate
next to last

Penultimate verses hold morals
So let's hastily finish these quarrels.
    No matter my feeling,
    Our country needs healing.
Let's earn us some peacemaker's laurels.

~ 101 ~

Tart
Sour or piquant

This collection of limericks tart
Was intended to make Trumpkins smart.
    While we vented our spleen
    At their rantings obscene,
We are freedom's defenders at heart.

The Authors
of the Limericks

The Authors of the Limericks

STEVE BENKO composed limericks #
1, 3, 4, 5, 6, 7, 8, 9, 10, 11, 12, 17, 18, 19, 20, 21, 22, 23, 24, 26, 28, 29, 30, 31, 33, 34, 35, 36, 37, 38, 40, 42, 43, 47, 48, 49, 53, 54, 56, 57, 58, 59, 61, 62, 63, 64, 66, 67, 69, 70, 71, 73, 77, 78, 90, and 91

PHIL GRAHAM is responsible for #
13, 14, 15, 16, 25, 27, 39, 52, 65, 68, 75, 79, 80, 82, 83, 84, 85, and 93

ZELDA DVORETZKY perpetrated #
2, 32, 41, 44, 45, 46, 50, 51, 55, 60, 74, 76, 81, 87, 94, and 95

And blame **LINDSAY CRANE** for #
72, 86, 88, 89, 92, 96, 97, 98, 99, 100, and 101

The Authors of the Limericks
are the following four
previously gruntled poets

LINDSAY CRANE is a psychologist, editor, grammar grinch, hot-headed activist, and author of a thriller (*The Lie-Catcher in the Primate House*).

STEVE BENKO is a recovering corporate middle manager, regular limericist, actor and producer on the local stage, and cat cuddler at the Connecticut Humane Society.

PHIL GRAHAM is a retired computer consultant and irrepressible punster. His blog, The Limericist, contains over 2,400 of his 5-liners, some clean and some "philthy."

ZELDA DVORETZKY has been a teacher, copywriter, publicist, and opera chorister. Now retired, she is a school volunteer and late-blooming poet.